Why Is This Festival Special?

Christmas

Jillian Powell

A⁺

Smart Apple Media

First published in 2005 by Franklin Watts
96 Leonard Street, London EC2A 4XD

Franklin Watts Australia
Level 17/207 Kent Street, Sydney NSW 2000

Series editor: Sarah Peutrill, Art director: Jonathan Hair, Designer: Ian Thompson,
Picture researcher: Diana Morris, Consultant: Martin Ganeri O.P.

Picture credits: A1pix: 21t. APL/ArkReligion: 20b. Bill Bachman/ImageWorks/
Topham: 24t. Peter Barker/Eye Ubiquitous: 22b. Sean Clayton/ImageWorks/Topham:
12. Andy Crawford: 15. Bob Daemmrich/ImageWorks/Topham: 6. Jeff Greenberg/
ImageWorks/Topham: 25t, 26b. E. James/ArkReligion: 13b. Mary Jeliffe/ArkReligion:
18. Perry Joseph: 17b. Nancy Durrell Mckenna/Hutchison: 17t. Jef Maion/Nomad's
Land/Alamy: 25b. Ray Moller: 10t, 11, 14, 20t, 21c, 21b, 23, 24b. Picturepoint/
Topham: 26c. Helene Rogers/ArkReligion: 7b, 8. Steve Mary Skjold/Eye Ubiquitous:
27. Liba Taylor/Hutchison: front cover t. A. Tjagny-rjadno/ArkReligion: 19b.
Topham: 7t. World Religions Picture Library: 3, 9bl, 9tr, 10b, 13t, 16, 22c.
World Religions Picture Library/Alamy: 19t.

Published in the United States by Smart Apple Media
2140 Howard Drive West, North Mankato, Minnesota 56003

U.S. publication copyright © 2007 Smart Apple Media

Library of Congress Cataloging-in-Publication Data

Powell, Jillian.
Christmas / by Jillian Powell.
p. cm. — (Why is this festival special?)
Includes index.
ISBN-13 : 978-1-58340-945-9
1. Christmas—Juvenile literature. I. Title.

GT4985.5.P69 2005
394.2663—dc22   2005051619

9 8 7 6 5 4 3 2 1

Contents

A special birthday 6

The Christmas story 8

Advent 10

Carols and plays 12

Christmas decorations 14

Christmas Eve 16

Going to church 18

Christmas presents 20

Festive food 22

Family time 24

The message of Christmas 26

Glossary 28

Christianity 29

Index 30

A special birthday

Christmas is a Christian festival.

Christians are people who follow a religion called Christianity. They live in countries all over the world and believe in one God.

Christians also believe that God sent Jesus Christ, His son, to the world to love and teach people and to save them from their sins. Christmas is the celebration of the birth of Jesus and is a happy time.

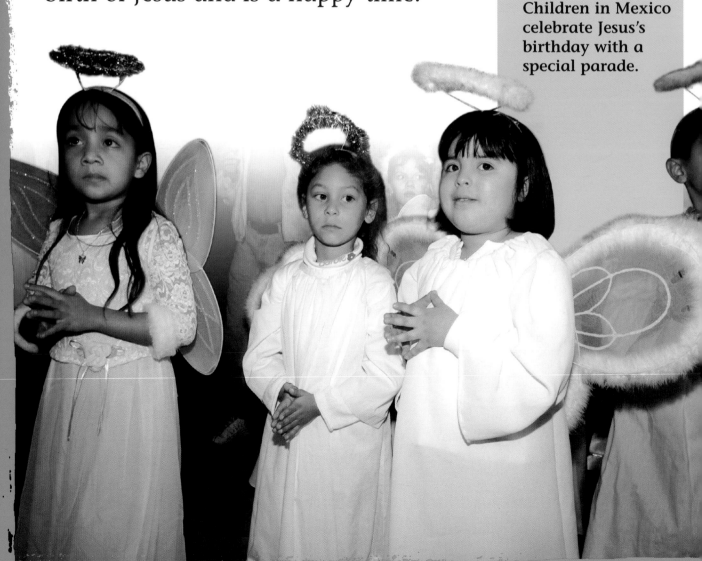

Children in Mexico celebrate Jesus's birthday with a special parade.

Christmas Day is celebrated once a year around the world. For many Christians, it is celebrated on December 25, but some people celebrate it on the 6th or 7th of January.

Christians in Ethiopia celebrating Christmas with a procession on January 7.

All over the world, families celebrate Christmas with a special meal.

Many people who are not Christian also celebrate Christmas. It is a time for all families to come together. Families share festive meals and give each other Christmas cards and gifts.

"At Christmas, we have a big family party at my grandma's house, and I get to play with all my cousins."

Max, age 10

The Christmas story

At Christmas, Christians remember the story of Jesus's birth.

The Christmas story tells how the angel Gabriel appeared to Mary. The angel told her she was going to give birth to a baby boy, who would be the Son of God.

Mary was engaged to be married to Joseph. When she was about to have her baby, they had to travel to Bethlehem for a census.

> **❝** *I did a drawing at school of the angel Gabriel.* **❞**
> *Nathan, age 10*

The Christmas story is shown in paintings and in stained glass windows in churches. This window shows Mary and the baby Jesus.

When Mary and Joseph reached Bethlehem, they could not find anywhere to stay and had to take shelter in a stable. Mary gave birth to Jesus in the stable and laid Him in a manger.

An angel brought news of Jesus's birth to shepherds.

The Three Wise Men gave the baby Jesus gifts of gold, frankincense, and myrrh.

When Jesus was born, an angel appeared to shepherds in the fields near Bethlehem. The angel told them God's son had been born, and the shepherds went to visit Him.

Three Wise Men saw a new star in the sky and followed it to find the baby Jesus, too.

Advent

Advent is the time when Christians look forward to Jesus's birth.

It begins four Sundays before Christmas Day. Children can count down the days to Christmas with an Advent calendar.

An Advent calendar marking each day with a scene or symbol of Christmas, such as a star.

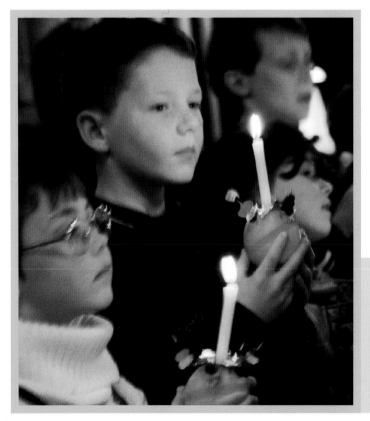

Many Christians go to church during Advent to sing carols and think about the Christmas story. Some carol services, called Christingles, are held by candlelight.

Children at a Christingle service. They hold an orange, which stands for the world, with a candle, which stands for the light Jesus brought into the world.

Nativity scenes are set up in churches, public places, and homes to remind people of the Christmas story.

> **"** *Mom lets me set up our Nativity scene every year. That's when I start to get excited because I know Christmas is coming.* **"**
> *Natalie, age 9*

People send cards to each other during Advent to wish each other "Merry Christmas."

There are lots of different card designs to choose from.

Carols and plays

The Christmas story is told in songs and plays.

During Advent and Christmas, Christians sing carols and play music to celebrate Jesus's birth. Carol singers visit people at home, singing and sometimes collecting money to give to poor and homeless people.

> " *I used to like singing carols around the crib when I was little.* "
> *Michelle, age 9*

Children singing Christmas carols.

In schools in America and other countries, young children perform in Nativity plays, acting out the Christmas story. Their parents and friends come to watch them.

Children dressed as Mary, the Wise Men, and the angels for a school Nativity play.

In Mexico, children go to the houses of friends and neighbors to sing songs and act out scenes from the Christmas story called *posadas*. The last house they visit takes them in, and after prayers, they have a party.

A girl carries a Nativity scene from house to house for the *posadas* in San Miguel, Mexico.

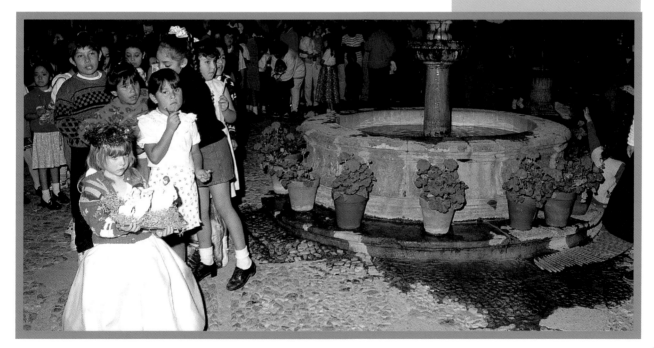

Christmas decorations

Decorations make homes, streets, stores, and churches look festive for Christmas.

People hang decorations and put up Christmas trees and twinkle lights in homes, stores, schools, and offices.

Candles and holly, ivy, and mistletoe are traditional decorations in homes and churches.

Holly and ivy wreaths are hung from front doors to welcome friends at Christmas.

Ornaments and other decorations reflect the lights on Christmas trees.

Towns and cities have colorful lights and Christmas trees in their main streets and squares.

In many towns and cities, colorful lights are hung over the main shopping streets.

A giant Christmas tree made from twinkle lights.

"My dad takes me to see the Christmas lights in town every year. They look really bright and cheerful."

Amy, age 9

In southern India, Christian families light small oil lamps and put them on the flat roofs of their houses.

Christmas Eve

In some countries, the biggest celebrations take place on Christmas Eve.

Christmas Eve is the night before Christmas. Many Christians go to church at midnight to celebrate the birth of Jesus.

At midnight, many Christians welcome Christmas with a service called Mass or Holy Communion.

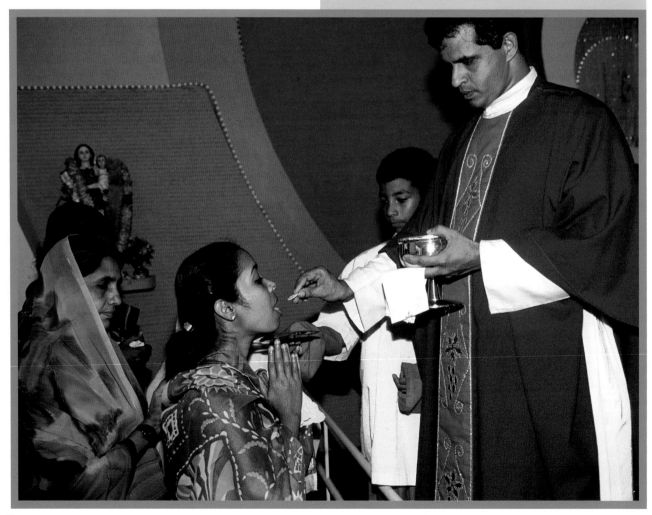

In Spain, people celebrate with street processions on Christmas Eve. They carry torches and play drums, tambourines, and guitars.

A Christmas Eve procession carries a statue of Mary and Jesus through a village in southern Spain.

In European countries such as Poland, Belgium, and Sweden, families celebrate with a special meal on Christmas Eve.

In Poland, it is traditional to start eating when the first star appears in the sky.

In Poland, families leave a place for the baby Jesus at the table on Christmas Eve.

Going to church

Many Christians go to church to celebrate Christmas.

All around the world, churches are full on Christmas Day with people celebrating the birth of Jesus.

> *" We go to church on Christmas morning. My sister sings in the choir there. "*
>
> *Hannah, age 9*

A village church in Fiji on Christmas Day.

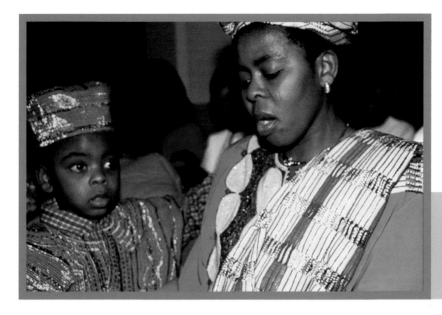

A family service in England on Christmas Day.

Many churches hold family services on Christmas Day. Families listen to the Christmas story from the Bible, and the priest or minister talks about the meaning of Christmas.

Children sometimes join in singing carols around a crib. People say prayers to thank God for the birth of Jesus. They pray for peace on Earth and for everyone who is poor, homeless, or sick.

A priest leads a Christmas service in a church in Moscow, Russia.

Christmas presents

Christmas is a time for giving and receiving presents.

The presents remind people of the gifts of gold, frankincense, and myrrh that the Three Wise Men gave to Jesus. They also remind Christians that God gave the world the gift of His only son, Jesus.

Presents wrapped up to be opened on Christmas Day.

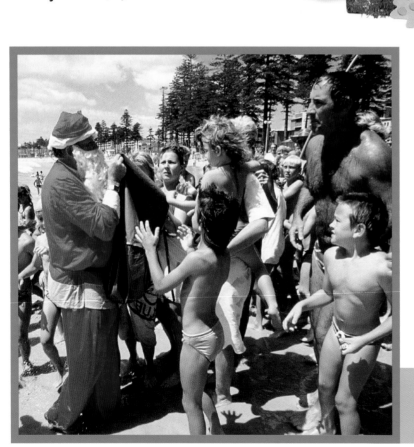

There are different traditions of who brings children their Christmas presents. In many countries, it is Santa Claus, who is also called Father Christmas, or Saint Nicholas who brings the presents.

Santa Claus visiting children on a beach in Australia.

In Germany, it may be the baby Jesus who brings presents; in Spain, the Wise Men; and in Italy, an old woman named La Befana.

This is a model of La Befana. Italian tradition says she brings gifts on the eve of January 6.

Presents may be left in Christmas stockings, shoes, or boots by a fireplace. Or they may be put under the Christmas tree.

Christmas stockings filled with presents ready for opening.

“ *On Christmas morning, I always find a sock at the foot of my bed filled with oranges, nuts, and very small presents. I get bigger presents later in the day.* ”

Callum, age 9

Festive food

Christmas is a time for feasting with family and friends.

At midday or in the evening, many families sit down for a big Christmas meal together. In the Czech Republic, even pets and farm animals share the Christmas food!

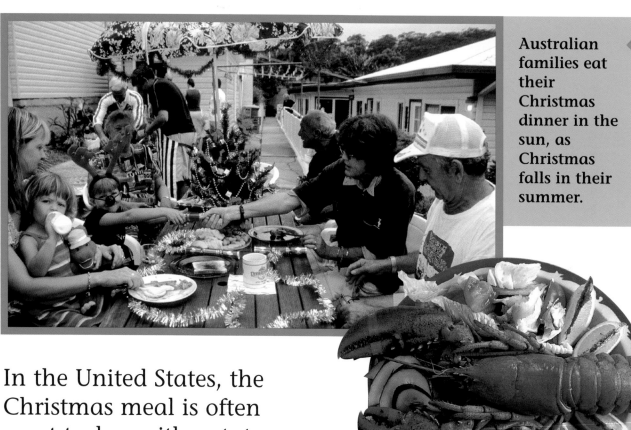

Australian families eat their Christmas dinner in the sun, as Christmas falls in their summer.

In the United States, the Christmas meal is often roast turkey with potatoes and vegetables. In Portugal, people eat salted dried codfish and potatoes, and in Nova Scotia, people eat lobster for Christmas dinner.

Lobster is a favorite Christmas dish in Nova Scotia, Canada.

People eat special desserts, too.

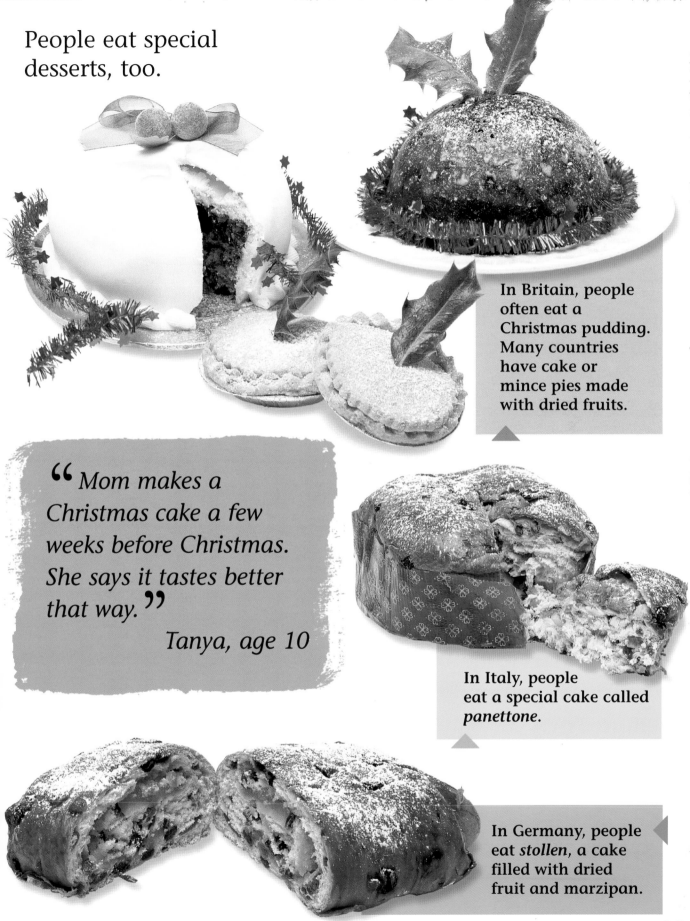

In Britain, people often eat a Christmas pudding. Many countries have cake or mince pies made with dried fruits.

" Mom makes a Christmas cake a few weeks before Christmas. She says it tastes better that way. "

Tanya, age 10

In Italy, people eat a special cake called *panettone*.

In Germany, people eat *stollen*, a cake filled with dried fruit and marzipan.

Family time

For many people, Christmas is a family time.

People travel home to spend Christmas with their family. Trains, planes, and roads get busy in the days before Christmas.

> Three generations of a family gather together to open their Christmas presents around the tree.

Families find many different ways to have fun at Christmas. Many families play games together at home.

" We always use noise-makers at Christmas. You pull them, and they make a loud bang. You find a hat to wear and a small toy or game inside. "

Lauren, age 9

Some families watch special Christmas parades.

A Christmas parade in Virginia.

At Christmas in Finland, people like to remember their loved ones who have died. They take candles to put on their family graves.

Candles brighten up graves in Finland at Christmas.

The message of Christmas

Christmas is a time for giving and caring. It is also a time for praying for peace on Earth.

At Christmas, Christians remember that Jesus taught them to love and care for each other, and to help those who are in need.

On Christmas Day, many people give their time to help others by taking food or gifts to people who are old, sick, or poor.

A boy takes a Christmas gift to an elderly neighbor.

These children are receiving toys collected for poor families by the police department.

Children help serve Christmas meals to homeless people at a soup kitchen.

At shelters and church halls, people cook and serve Christmas meals for the poor and homeless.

Around the world, Christians pray for an end to war and for forgiveness and peace in all countries. This was the message that the angels sang to the shepherds at Jesus's birth.

" At the club I go to after church on Sundays, we wrapped up boxes of food to take to old people who live nearby. "

Daniel, age 10

Glossary

Advent the four weeks before Christmas.

Bethlehem the town, south of Jerusalem in Israel, where Jesus was born.

Bible the holy book of Christianity.

carol a song sung at Christmas to celebrate the birth of Jesus.

census a count of people. In Roman times, people and their property were counted for taxation.

Christingle a candle held in an orange, which is decorated with a red ribbon and other fruit or nuts.

Communion when Christians eat blessed bread and wine. They do this in memory of Jesus and of all that he did for them. Many Christians believe Jesus is present after the bread and wine are blessed. The service in which Communion takes place is called by a number of names, such as the Mass, Holy Communion, the Last Supper, and the Eucharist.

crib a baby's bed, with high sides.

frankincense a perfume that comes from trees.

manger a long box that holds hay for feeding animals.

myrrh a perfume that comes from trees.

Nativity play a play that tells the story of Jesus's birth.

Nativity scene a model of the scene in the stable when Jesus was born.

sins bad or wrong actions, thoughts, or behavior.

Christianity

Christianity is one of the world's main religions. There are more than one billion Christians around the world. Christians believe in one God, who made everything in the universe.

Jesus Christ

Christians follow the teachings of Jesus Christ, who lived about 2,000 years ago. They believe that Jesus is the Son of God and that He was sent to save people from sin and death. Jesus taught people to love and praise God as their Father, and to love and care for others. Jesus was crucified (killed on a wooden cross). Christians believe He came back to life on the third day after His death and that everyone who believes in Him will live again after they die.

Christian lives

Christians are christened, or baptized, to show that they believe in Jesus. They follow the teachings of the holy Bible and praise God with hymns, readings from the Bible, and prayers.

Branches

Christians belong to different branches. These include the Roman Catholic, Orthodox, Anglican, Pentecostal, Methodist, and Baptist branches, and many others.

Festivals

Christmas is an important festival for most Christians, but there are many other important Christian festivals in the year, including Easter.

Index

Advent 10, 11, 12, 28
Advent calendar 10

Befana, La 21
Bible 19, 28, 29

candles 10, 14, 25, 28
carols 10, 12, 19, 28
Christian 6, 7, 8, 10, 12,
    15, 16, 18, 20, 26, 27,
    28, 29
Christianity 6, 28, 29
Christmas Day 7, 10, 18,
    19, 20, 26
Christmas Eve 16, 17
Christmas story 8, 9, 10,
    11, 12, 13, 19
church 8, 10, 14, 16, 18,
    19, 27
Communion 16, 28

decorations 14

Father Christmas 20
food 13, 22, 23, 26, 27

gifts 7, 9, 20, 21, 26

Jesus 6, 8, 9, 10, 12, 16,
    17, 18, 19, 20, 21, 26,
    27, 28, 29
Joseph 8

light 10, 14, 15

meals 7, 17, 22, 27
Midnight Mass 16
music 12

Nativity 11, 13, 28

parade 6, 25
peace 19, 26, 27
posadas 13
prayers 13, 19, 29
presents see gifts

Santa Claus 20
shepherds 9, 27

Wise Men 9, 13, 20, 21